Paris–Forfar

To Gerry

With every best wish
and looking forward
to lots more flying)

from David

Paris–Forfar

David Kinloch

Polygon
EDINBURGH

Published by Polygon
22 George Square
Edinburgh

Set in Sabon by Koinonia Ltd,
Manchester
Printed and bound in Great Britain by
Short Run Press Ltd, Exeter

A CIP record is available

ISBN 0 7486 6183 2

The Publisher acknowledges subsidy
from the Scottish Arts Council towards
the production of this volume.

For Mum and Eric

Départ dans l'affection et le bruit neufs!

Flittin i fire-edge an spleet-new bellum!
                    Arthur Rimbaud

Acknowledgements

Acknowledgements and thanks are due to the editors of the following magazines and anthologies where some of these poems first appeared:
Angel Exhaust, *Cencrastus*, *The Crazy Jig*, *Dream State: The New Scottish Poets*, *Gairfish*, *The Jacarandah Review*, *Lines Review*, *London Magazine*, *The New Makars*, *New Writing Scotland*, *Object Permanence*, *Spectrum* and *Verse*.

'The Clinic' was a prizewinner in the Poems made manifest competition, 1992.

Part 1 of *Dustie-Fute* first appeared from Vennel Press in 1992.

Note: The short prose poems in Scots (*Dustie-Fute*) are adaptations from the Portuguese of Eugenio de Andrade's *Memória Doutro Rio*.

Readers will find individual lyrics in Scots glossed for their convenience at the foot of the page. However, the Scots words scattered throughout the three-part sequence of poems, *Dustie-Fute* are meant to be less easily assimilable and definitions may be found in the glossary at the end of the volume.

Four friends in particular helped to make these poems happen: thanks to Robert Crawford, Bill Herbert, Donny O'Rourke and Richard Price for their constant encouragement.

Contents

2 HECKIEBIRNIE

3 DR DAVID KYNALOCHUS IN LE PENSIONNAT D'HUMMING-BIRD GARDEN

THE REV. ROBERT WALKER SKATING ON DUDDINGSTON LOCH

The water tensed at his instruction
and trout gazed up at his incisive feet.
We felt that God must be in clarity like this
and listened to the dull glens echo
the striations of his silver blades.

Far out on Duddingston loch
our true apostle sped
with twice the speed of Christ
who walked on waves.

We saw him harrow ice
with grace of the elect
and scar the transubstantiation
of wintered elements.

With a sense of real presence
he crossed our loch
what need of vestments
with such elegant legs?

REX

I think I am Charles the first,
lopped, rolling towards my Scottish blood,
wild honey for Roundheads.

I connect nothing with nothing:
the Puritan natural life is gone
with its oranges, its moon,
its scriptural vocatives

of court and country pleasantness.
They bring up the box
and place my countries in it;
they will have space to cool.

REVOLUTION

Revolution
brought a thaw to the silver structure
of snow in Glasgow

and my father climbed
the hill of our garden
carrying a tree.
Its branches antlered him,
warlock with a broom he planted
upside down.

We planted a pear tree
under which our moles
spun grass into still
whirlpools of blade and seed.
My feet just small enough to fit
tripped on their volcanic lips.

Revolution:
this morning my father swallowed
sixteen coloured pills from bottles
and pointed to a pear tree
bearing fruit he cannot go to pick.

His arms which carried trees
have dimples at their elbows,
moles hills of flesh
with wrinkled lips,
his head as smooth
as the youngest pear leaf.

fruitfall in the grass
drowns the faintest footfall
going to gather earth

INTERFLORA

Iris, lupin, varieties of bell
flower, slip through my ribbed voice
wishing you a cataract of blue,
dialling flora, weaving vegetable
wires from here to Glasgow.

They loop in to you,
long-necked, deep yellow-throated,
pearl lobes or pear tongues on stilts.
I forget the listening florist

and introduce through perforated
holes of your mouthpiece,
shy, insistent petals.

My flower voice steps into
your Vermeer room,
muddying with peaty leaves
its pale, clean light.

It arranges you about linoleum
or sandalwood, you in your iris
smock beneath a map of the unfinished world,

places your hands like vases
on the television set, a crystal
light flickering to their tips
and nails from earthed wrists
in Katrine tap-water.

Its green conversation
tenders you and you grow on
into the parched Erskine night.

I hope you are dreaming
only of florists' doorbells.
Before sleep I see only
the receiving cradle of your arms.

EPITHALAMIUM
for Nick and Cynthia

In the accuracy of a steady northern room,
a minnow-flamed candle
electrolyses bacteria of light.
Clyde-boned, I shelve Vermeer's blue map
of Europe which once meant 'the open space',
a palingenesis of old-world freeways,
and consult the Melbourne temperature.

Hands soft from touching recent globes,
I wait for day to marry with its first gilt rings
the mercantile lead casements of this house,
then take pith of epithalamium and send it to you,
imagining the rising threshold
of Australian light and its wedding with space begin.

Fur shining in the Glasgow mizzle,
Vermeer's geographer wishes you this morning
a glimpse of James Cook
substantiating in astonishment
the plain light straw colour
of a new pacific land.

ROOBRUB

Whan roobrub wiz greengown corrock
than eh swuffit easy, a slibbie grawl
papplin i a hammock o air,
meh tail a swingin-tree;
roobrub wiz a sky yawl
shapit lyk a cloud.

Morn-i-e-mornin,
doon i the moor-band
tongue-deavin the liquory stem,
eh wiz the Hopi o roobrub teepee,
tent-preachin o worm-web,
scripture o cunyie-mirk, muck an green licht.

Dayligaun, whan eh gave lug
tae her cup, she wiz roarin-buckie,
an root atween legs,
leaf flauchterin navel,
eh plumpit the further o munes,
shell-gowd pap-o-the-hass.

When I lay as a child on a rhubarb leaf, as in a virgin green basket, then I breathed and scuttled like a slippery young salmon, bubbling in a hammock of air, my tail a flail; rhubarb was a sky boat shaped like a cloud. In the early morning down in the peaty earth deafening with a loud tongue the sweet-toothed stem, I was the Hopi of a rhubarb teepee, preaching in open air of cobweb, a scripture of smugness, muck and green light. At sundown when I put my ear to the cupped leaves, a fishing trap, she was roaring-buckie (a kind of shell), then, tucking the stalk between my legs, leaf quivering over navel, I plunged into a future of moons, gold leaf uvula.

8

BLINK
eftir Eugenio de Andrade

Na, it's no yit the fykie
licht o Mairch
at the neb o a smirk,
nor the greeshoch speil o the bere,

a shot-star o swalla
showerickie
at a nakit shouder,
a smaa lane burn nid-noddy
i its thrapple;

na, nor the guid, tairt guff
o the body, eftir luve,
snakin doun-by tae the tide,
or the doukin lown

o the peerie yaird,
lik a yawl wi a smirk at its neb;

na, it's jist a blink.

fykie–troublesome, difficult. neb–nose, the beak of a bird.
greeshoch–red, glowing, flameless fire. bere–barley.
shot-star–meteor. swalla–swallows. showerickie–slight or
gentle shower. thrapple–throat. lown–soft. peerie–small.
yawl–boat. blink–instant, moment.

i.m. JOAN EARDLEY

The sea is a wall.
There is no latticework of air among the waves,
Only tenemented stone
Rigid with desire to breathe.

Childrens' faces poke from it,
Shadowed pebbles, flakes
Of slate chips
Chattering in the sea.

One thinks she has seen a beautiful shell
In Tillie Street:
A small boy lifts up
Triumphant broken glass.

The wall is a sea.
Its waves pretend a light and midnight breeze
That breathe of their desire
To build children from its crumbling shell.

REFUGEE

Hand bells rang bombers out of the Tighnabruaich
Sky; another lesson after the break
For Clydebank evacuees.

Children could not get used to their streetwise
Brassy slap: my father woke expecting mathematics,
The taste of school-milk in his ears.

Now he hands me his last will,
Basildon Bond smudged by a screech
Of brakes,

A cancer in his shoulder blade,
Humming like a blue train,
Ready to depart.

THE TEAR IN PAT KANE'S VOICE

The tear in Pat Kane's voice
Offers you the shadow of a bi-plane
Unutterably high just next to silence:

Off the grain, it thinks more quickly
Than the images of his songs
And each true thought concludes
In the break where each true note begins.

The tear in Pat Kane's voice
Offers you a man's name,
Whiter and harder than Alba:

Adorno at his plain table,
Rubbing out the barbaric lyrics
Of post-Auschwitz poets

And cleansed children,
Desperately seeking a river crossing
In a blown-up ferry,
While we sit like empty cars
In a reconverted bauble,
Crossing from one song to
Another over the nailed--down waves.

SECOND INFANCY

'We've washed her', said the nurse.
And then we met a bank of sour carbolic air,
My grandmother hovering in a tiny wicker basket,
A gossamer mesh of rib and hair
Caught on its interstices.

Suddenly I remembered that trip with her
To Greenock, the smack she gave me
For imprinting a ring of muck around my eye
When I pressed it to whorls in the pier,
Trying to see the sea.

And later, on the boat, as I pulled towards me
Her cats-cradle, the game that always made
The shape of her forgiveness,
She kissed me, as I kiss her now.

Looking down through the criss-cross cot,
She seems to gently see-saw
As we did once on disused gangways,
And in the evening light, threaded
Between the latticework, I briefly see
Cold waves through the dark rings of my eyes.

THE KURNAI

Chew quietly, do not offend the Sun:
MacMillan of Cuillin, a lightning corpse
sprung shining from Wunger mountains,

Mraat, a peeled fruit from white tuber,
stunted by the vicious clearance of his kingdom.

They stood to attention as he named
the fishful waterways: Caledonia Australis.

The Child had come to live with them;
they listened, laughing, to Lorne bells at his back,

the simple hymns of green hills far away
and shared edible insects, gaudy birds of the air.

At Warrigal Creek Gaels built a static catherine wheel
of Kurnai bones and skulls.

Black widows went back to thistle land
dancing with Lochaber rabbits.
Boil fish, they cried to children, appease the Moon.

WOMEN
after Yannis Ritsos

They are so far away, the women. Their sheets smell of
  bonne nuit.
They place bread on the table so that we do not feel their
  absence.
Then we understand that we have done something wrong.
We get up and we say:
'You've tired yourself out today', or else, 'Leave it. I'll light
  the lamp'.
When we strike the match, she turns away slowly and
  moves
as if by some inexplicable attraction towards the kitchen.
Her back is a bitter little mountain laden with many deaths:
family deaths, her own private deaths, and you with them.
You hear her footsteps creak the old boards,
you hear the dishes crying on the washboard, and then it's
the train taking the soldiers to the front.

ODE TO HART CRANE

The *Orizaba's* havana bark
sherried the warm waters
you were set upon;

a horizontal Christmas tree
gingerly crushing the ocean's crepe
its conifer lights needled you

to the edge of the Bridge.

From a space-invader on Mumbles pier
I plot your dolphin trajectory,
that crazy cakewalk

over the suspended blue blue air
into the plummet of your laugh:
it lobs on my screen like an ode.

Today my pier which embraced with wood
the curve of Swansea bay
and talked me beyond your rainbow words

is drift along the shore.

Brooklyn Bridge will feel its touch
when the sly sea wells again
with shavings of your Cuban ark.

THE VOYAGE
for Donny O'Rourke

Baudelaire's mother sent him to sea
To cure him of the vice of verse.

But at Saint-Denis de Bourbon
He tried to disembark

Through rough waves to a sea-saw
Jetty with selected Balzac

Tucked beneath his arm.

Through twelve feet of ocean
The poet climbed the small boat's

Ladder but in the elevator
Of Mauritian water

Found himself alone at last
With the Human Comedy,

Swept up in its mane of emerald eyes,
Heard poems swimming striped

And suddenly yellow in his brain,
Then stepped like Aphrodite

Up to dry land, books fast
But opening in his hands.

ICARUS

Finding a smile in a blue quill
at fifty thousand feet
you chased its infant vertigo
up the shiver of a feather

and at the tip
discovered in the pearly spine
a reflection of your eyes:
nesting water chestnuts laughing
back at you with a desire
that split the sky blue quill.

Falling in the box room
of your wings, you examine
every feathered wall,
each blue smile
the split quill spills,

the justice of the tiny
wheels and cogs of sunlight
cancelling their beams.

And now in a sky blue sea
the quills of pleasant shellfish
suck smiles from your bones,
feathers of buried sunlight
ghosting in your eyes.

TO GLYN MAXWELL

Glyn. This noun could be a verb
but all poets names are or aspire to be;
'to glyn', close to 'glean' which is what
all poets do or aspire to do, or
close to 'gleam' and transforming,
gathering, polishing is what we do
or are supposed to do according to
our betters and the comforting homonyms
our names suggest.

Glyn, glean, gleam, however you look
at it, I keep hoping I will find a
glen in what I write and who I write it to,
a homely source, a 'region of short distances
and definite places', spring water in your name.

But Glasgow, simply a step along
a shuttle's dim and droning evening corridor,
is just wings of familiar accents
gliding through the lunar beauty
of thirty thousand feet, mere talk
in space, our home: the gleam of writing 'speed'.

ICARUS
after Robert Desnos

Somewhere Eskimos are weeping
For failing to bury enough sunlight
In their igloos.
But in Outer-Siberia a man with a bear-skin
Telescope laughs like the steppe,
Detecting the changing smiles of Icarus
At different pitches of the air.

'THE USUAL SUSPECTS', 19/4/94
for Jackie Kay

Slim, black and silver mike,
You have found us out.
We must be deft, debate
Varieties of love: '3, 2, 1':
'Umm   ah ', '*Passé?*!'.
It killed him and he isn't
Hiding in the headphones' cave.

Jackie, you tell them 'I'
Aint necessarily 'me'
But in this so still, so listening quiet,
I can hear the twisted
Coral of your earring
Graze your cheek and
Feel the Judas in me as I agree.

Later, alone, listening to us 'live',
I hear me tell the whole
Of Scotland that I love him.
Straight. The only way.

SONGS FOR ALAN BRECK

i
His grin broke-dance the club
Like an ice-cream headache:

I played Mr Betwixt and Between
And loved the careless way
He decanted eyebrows
Into his whisky glass,

Tipping them at last
To catch my smile
Dissolving in their distance.

Guinea-loined –
O Charlemagne Breck –
He cut me with the gaelic
Whistle that named surprise,
Our first and only lowland date.

ii
And when he lunged at me that night, half in anger, half in
playfulness it was as if Kinlochaline and Kingairloch were all
one to me and in me and that we were both caught up, as it
were, in the restrictive exaltation of a special rhythm that is
poetry itself, a high country, indeed, as sharp as a pen. That
night, my Alan was all of Appin, the grand sonority, James of
the Glens and John of the Claymore and with his forehead
pressed to mine sweat beads pricked out his eyebrows like a
net of lemons to brew punch with.

iii
He caught up with me in a bellibucht although I believe in his

country it was the custom to call a hollow in a hill such as we presently found ourselves in a glack. He searched me like a chamber with kisses. 'Where the fuck have you been? I've been thinking you were lost to me foreffer, you wee tyke!' And so I explained to my dear friend that my bed had been the moorcock, that I had taigled many a weary foot and he for his part had seen me and lost me and seen me again as I tumbled in the roost. 'Och David man! I saw one man go down like a pair of breeks. My mind has been every conceivable variety of marsh since you went from me'. 'Aye', said I, 'I have been bobbin-quaw too without you, and flush and flow. My loins have been laggery for you but I have plowtered through. But Alan, darling, be quick moss to my shoggie bog now. Come, let's make transmeridiane of this sluch.'

iv
He was the ait-seed i the icker,
Hid in a glans of corn,
An end-pickle waving in wind
From the heugh of the Corrynakeigh.

Promiscuous and sassy,
The redcoats stopped to pluck him,
Slapped his stalk
On easy thighs
Through the hot June beat.

Whipped through air
I nestled to him,
Oxter pickle in the
Husk and then at dusk
The soldier sucked
And tossed us in the heather.

MAKING HAY

Cutting grass, I used to drive Dad
Wild. He would align me with the topmost
Tree and at my crazy zig-zag
Smash his hand against his brow
And say it was deliberate.

Truth is, I loved to leave
Substantial lines of Indian
Scalp two feet or so apart.
Today, a small boy smiles up
At me, his tiny bike abandoned
By our neat parterre, listening
In glee to enraged dog turd
Whip around the blades.

Now I get it straight
For all the 'neighbours'
Who come from round the block
Just to watch us cut the grass:
Me mowing, him hoeing up the hay.

I smile at them as at the old
Crail lady who used to man
Her garden gate each morning
Just to see me smile,
'A special smile' she said.

THE RETREAT

My room was a foggy Patmos
Hung high in the Devon night.

In its island light I hugged my knees
And listened to a priest confess

My friend who lay protectively next door.

Then I saw the tiny snout-nosed
Virgin leaping from the wall,

Burrying humbly through my bed,
Seeking my freezing feet.

I heard the gentle belch of Buckfast
Monks in their library of grapes;

I closed my eyes wishing their tonic
Wine would cure me of retreat

And listened for the sound
Of Baskerville's legendary hound

Which lay on the ridge beyond.

In sleep it came: the mocking
Rastafarian of a fellow oblate

Who'd cried 'Conversion!' at me.
And then I woke, knowing that I loved

My friend.

QUASIMODO

Was it the infinite vertigo of the smiling griffin that made the little hump grow? Stone suddenly becoming aware of air, of its own violent shape? As the queue got smaller I could feel the back-muscles bunch, a gathering and a lifting until I sailed up the tower of Notre-Dame, a Montgolfier balloon of laughter and perception. My fingers trace in the walls a graffiti of tiny humps, the words *murs bossus* flowering into tourists bending double as they clamber up or down. Compressed sap in a tree of stone, every blood-group known to man rises into a fountain of snapping cameras. Green saints cling to the spire. Below, across the Seine, is the little studio where I lived my 19th year. That's where the hump began to grow – as I gazed at these towers where I stand now. Bring out your humps I say! Let humps flourish! In Glasgow and Paris and Forfar and Leon. In New York and Boulogne and Bordeaux. Inexplicably you place your hands on the parapet before me: iris laid against this balustrade like an illuminated psalm, blue palms from the air, asking me to walk upon them freshly to a calvary of sorts. Words receive me from their yellow throats. Words streaked with black, pencilled eyebrows, little rafts of darkness which I finger gently with my mind. I step into them and take the oar. When this immense violence leaves me as suddenly as a fever – to the moved surprise of my father always stroking my brow at that very instant – there is only this bearable caress for me and for you. Now the sun drives round a buttress as supple as a Rolls-Royce Silver Ghost with Rare Salamanca Coach Work. I, Quasimodo, step into it without sunglasses, divested of hat and parasol, all balms and lotions, my hunch-back naked to the burning wind. I, Quasimodo, lord of a new dance, chauffeur of fire and air.

DUSTIE-FUTE

To speak is to spin, and the thread weaves the world.

In the Andes, language itself, Quechua, derives from Keswa, a rope made of twisted grass, two people making love, many fibers in one.

Palley, to weave designs is to raise the fibers by picking them up.

To read in Latin, legere is to collect or pick up.

Cecelia Vincuña

When I opened my window and reached for the yoghurt cooling on the outside ledge, it had gone. All that remained was a single Scottish word bewildered by the Paris winter frost and the lights of its riverbank motorways. What can *dustie-fute* have to say to a night like this? How can it dangle on its hyphen down into the rue Geoffroy L'Ansier where Danton stayed on the eve of revolution? How can it tame this strangeness for me or change me into the cupolas and flag-stones I so desire yet still notice every time I walk among them? Does the 'auld alliance' of words and things stand a chance among the traffic and pimps in the Publicis Saint-Germain? For its not as if *dustie-fute* were my familiar. I could easily confuse *dustie-fute* with *elfmill* which is the sound made by a worm in the timber of a house, supposed by the vulgar to be preternatural. These words are as foreign as the city they have parachuted into, dead words slipping on the sill of a living metropolis. They are extremes that touch like dangerous wires and the only hope for them, for us, is the space they inhabit, a room veering between dilettantism and dynamite. Old Scots word, big French city and in be-tween abysmal me: *ane merchand or creamer, quha hes no certain dwelling place, quhair the dust may be dicht fra hes feete or schone*. Dustie-fute, a stranger, equivalent to *fairand-man*, at a loss in the empty soul of his ancestors' beautiful language and in the soulless city of his compeers living the 21st century now and scoffing at his medieval wares. Yet here, precisely here, is their rendez-vous and triumphantly, stuffed down his sock, an oblique sense, the dustie-fute of 'revelry', the acrobat, the juggler who accompanies the toe-belled jongleur with his merchant's comic fairground face. He reaches deep into his base latinity, into his *pede-pulverosi* and French descendants pull out their own *pieds poudreux*.

Dustie-fute remembers previous lives amid the plate glass of Les Halles. They magnify his motley, his midi-oranges, his hawker lyrics and for a second Beaubourg words graze Scottish glass then glance apart. In this revelry differences copulate, become more visible and bearable and, stranger than the words or city I inhabit, I reach for my yoghurt and find it there.

DRAUGHT O A GREEN CHIEL

He cam fae anither country, had kent thrist an the watter o
Mairch bere, his feet i the wey o thi slaw stour o eternitie.

The dour snaw cam eftir.

eftir Eugenio de Andrade

JOHN JAMIESON'S FIRST BILLY-GOAT PRIMER

OUTSIDE a goat is eating *Le Monde*. It is not on my map of
the many worlds of Ethiopia but it is there all the same,
slowly digesting the proche orient. Mitterand, pornographie,
un coup de dés, la terre, Addis Ababa, turn on its tongue like
printed matter. A starving goatherd hands me the map of this
country I have never been to. Its names flype his inside-out
pocket. Listen to Lalibela, Makalle, Debre Damo, Assab,
names which could be people, months, implements in their
places. On this white expanse their meaning catches in the
throat, dipping into a dictionary of a half-familiar tongue
which you knew in the life of a four million year old girl. The
goat in the margin has come to the small ads. The air is full of
voices selling and buying in unknown dialects. The thrill of
your *First ABC* given by Great AnTan seeps into your brain
like a sky-blue dye for the first time since the age of five. Here
is an A-Z of Ethiopia, a dictionary of the first land, word-
world of Prester John whose inaccessible court greenmantled
your childhood with anticipation. Now in its forgotten lan-
guage it is a small white nation, a night ship trawling its
estuaries for names it can inhabit with a smidgin of equanim-
ity. A. A is for Lake Abaya but also for the ae-fur-land,
precipitate, steep land which grounds you and will be
ploughed in one direction only: skywards without entering
the soil. A is for Asmara and for the accumie pen, that
metallic pencil prophets wrote in deserts with, that original
abstraklous pen that etched commandments into adder
beads. A for Axum and for the alamonti, the ever-moving
storm finch which meets you everywhere, ableeze in a tiny
bush of words. And beyond A is a great adventure. Go up
into the attic. There Grandmother is waiting, a yellow primer
in her arms. You are among the minnows and the Sunblest
packets and crushed daffodils breast-stroking the pond in a

Sabean dialect. You are sailing out on Lake Abaya and there in the middle distance see the rich loop, the dip and curl of a J, a Joram in a jockey coat, a boat song decked out in a greatcoat against the nippy weather, Joram with its blue shores, its intense bracken alive with a misery of midges. Listen. Through the mirage of half-remembered grammar my grandmother declines towards me from the desert shimmer:

Gow, gow-glentie,
Ee, ee brentie,
Mou, mou merry,
Cheek, cheek cherry,
Nose, nose nap,
Chin, chin chap.

Below us, the murloch swims, a very delicate fish with its rough skin of which it must be stripped. Close by the shore, boys are at galations, up the tenement closes in paper caps and sashes with wooden swords; mind the holsie-jolsie, the hubble, the gibble-gabble. Steek the gab! Hawk-study this parched tongue, furry with the things and places it is pointing to. The sky is thawing words, Chicken-Licken. They rain, they are fish. Fish them, eat them. Like the he-goat. Here is A again, A for aiver, the gelded billy-goat chewing yesterday's newspaper. And crouching by him for azmari, the shepherd's minstrel, the dustie-fute singing to us of the desert, who knows mostly about goats and words, sometimes confusing them like his charge which cannot tell the difference. The man is quiet, listening to his goat munch a herb. In Pliny it is called *aethiopus:* 'which is of a power, by touching only, to open locks, or unbolt any door'.

GURLIEWHIRKIE

Unforseen evil, dark, dismal, premeditated revenge. It is scarcely possible to know the origin of terms of such uncouth combination and indefinite meaning. Jamieson's Etymological Dictonary of the Scottish Tongue

Habbacraws! The Renfrew Ferry throws up its glass bonnet. She nods. Tonight she sails: blackfisher of the Clyde. Far out beneath the Kingston Bridge an illegal banquet cups its ears and jumping to its feet says: 'Can you hear them? I hear people in the air, but cannot see them. Listen!' We strain (with every pore) until we hear invisible brothers, whole words against our flesh. And they are: *greengown, dustiefute, rinker, rintherout, set, abstraklous, alamonti, afftak, baghash, amplefeyst, let-abee for let-abee.* It is dew on Gideon's fleece. It is Homer's bounding, flying and consequently alive words. It is Plato thawing in the Glasgow air. It is the head and lyre of Orpheus. All these and on the deck before us whole handfuls of frozen words, gay quips, some vert, some azure and some or. Shall we fear them then? Take no risks and we'll get no slaps! One of us begins to horde, yet, warmed between our hands, they crane upwards like a baby cham. It's then the gurliewhirkie gets to work: just as we're about to understand their throats are cut. Mump the cuddy, aftercome, falderall and ezle melt on a lover's palm and shout: hin, hin, hin, his, tock, tock, bou, bou, bou, bou, tracc, tr, trr, on, on, on, on, proddle, proop. Habbacraws! We saw them look back over our shoulder into the water. We saw the words stop bobbing like so many buoys in the water. We saw the last gleam of dark eyebrows in the water and it said: *by-coming, bairnie of the e'e.*

35

SANG O EPIRUS

Whit bydes stayedly i thi efternune, lik i thi sang o thi hirds o
Epirus, is an orange. Thi fit-staps are doused, thi name itsel is
lost, that slaw, skeer lowe, it wiz thi fore o lips or burds. An
orange. Whitely. I thi hauns o a bairn.

DUSTIE-FUTE IN MUMBLES

I get up in the night
And let his voice
Out of the breakwater into light.

Pier upon pier constellates
In the lyre of his memory:
Jetties tensing at the touch of boys' feet
Which echo in his mind like ships
That nudged his severed head, bobbing now
In my swivel chair like a buoy.

Dustie-fute released from the Oregon
Pine of Mumbles pier, tells me
Of mushroom anchors, jarrah wood paving
Of Dundee and how at Arromanches,
Locked within mild steel pontoons,
He took the weight of tanks.

Post-Euridice, he has floated in
To tell me of the sex of words
Which looped around his ears
Among difficult Scottish kyles,
Setting aucht upon his lips
Froe and huzziebaw in his hair.

He has come to tell me how domestic loss
Placed a cypress in his heart,
Its tongue half-learnt and half-inherited
Which gave fast stories that surged in him
Like lifts, sharp swords that hung above his head.

He has come to tell me of an underwater
Tongue, hippocamp, pure, useless
As the moles and dolphins
Which burrow and porpoise
Only in arcades of pleasure
They bear upon their backs.

EFTIR EUGENIO DE ANDRADE

A freen is whileoms widder-gleam,
whileons watter.
Lat gang thi dounmaist souch
o August; a body

isna ae thi ben o an auch,
nakit licht, o burd-
bouky birks,
summer-cloks i thi snood;

its i thi daurk fullyerie o sleep
that lytach flesh
sheens,
thi fykie lempitt-ebb o thi tongue.

Whit is rale is thi wurd.

THE LOVE THAT DARE NOT

Even the illness that extinguishes it comes in borrowed clothes, not one name but many, forming the syntax of your end. Unravelling its hidden meanings, side-stepping tears that dare not fall yet because they would admit the last page of this dictionary has been turned, I trace you back, nudging you, as I used to, from word to word:

the days you called me *rinker*, a tall, thin, long-legged horse, a bloody harridan, I called you *rintherout*, a gadabout, a needy, homeless vagrant, like the tongue we spoke beneath the sheets. Our life as mobile and happy as the half a dozen Scottish verbs I'd push across a page on Sunday afternoons, trying to select a single meaning.

Here it is: under *Ripple* or *Rippill*, a squat paragraph which tells us we must separate the seed of flax from the stalk, undo our badly-done work, separate and tear in pieces. And when we are birds, must eat grains of standing corn, when clouds, open up, disperse, clear off. Its noun has you in its grip: an instrument with teeth for rippling flax.

Or you might find us under *set* which seats, places hens on eggs in order to hatch them, assigns work, settles, gets in order; puts milk into a pan for the cream to rise, sets fishing-lines, works according to a pattern, plants potatoes, makes, impels, includes, besets, brings to a halt and puzzles, nause-ates, disgusts, marks game, lets, leases, sends, dispatches, becomes, suits, beseems, sits, ceases to grow, becomes ma-ture, stiffens, congeals, starts, begins, sets off

the love that dare not   Except that now, so near the end, when I would like to hold you and have been forbidden, I search for it in your eyes, daring their definition.

THE CLINIC

The clinic records false names
Assigns us leaflets and a Sister
Who calls us 'boys'. A doctor,
Briefly green and ponderous,
Assumes that 'friend' from my tongue
Is a euphemism, and poises pen
Above white boxes for supplementary
Non-grata. We are not here

Imagining instead a big breezy
Bed on Kingsbarns beach,
No need for bandages on hands
Where eczema leaves tiny pits
For love's curious virus.

No sweat. It is safe inside him,
Sealed by skin against sun and water,
A hermit cell among the cells
Which one day will strike out
From shore and evangelize.

DUSTIE-FUTE ON RHODOPE

His tongue is cypress on tiptoe
above a chattel of Ibizan bars
and his uncut nail a carbon wave
against an island sky.

His voice is groves of esh
and hoburn sauch,
his throat the knot-holes of their bark
which pestle the laughter
of a small port's clubs
with the ferryman's light scorn.

His eyes are a boy's chanter,
reedy as remote infantas,
his red and blue chirrups
balance air, lob through
the house-music from the bay.

His back is a woman
turning through the night
and women will turn on him.
His lips are a discus of hyacinth,
vernacular rooting in its fall.

His smile is an accent
stretched by Ciconian hordes.
until his limbs cartwheel away,
beche-de-mer, brogue,
caught in girls' hair
which streams the common
printout of their pain.

CREAM O THI WELL

Tae apen hauns. As if thi wun war thi mairvel. Tae straik thi outloup o his mane, lently thi lent fever craig. Tae lat him lae, still green. Wi thi outpour, cream o thi well.

eftir Eugenio de Andrade

HECKIEBIRNIE

three miles beyond hell (Jamieson)

PARIS-FORFAR

From the window of the Hardie-Condie Cafe, I see the ghost of a rich friend of my grandmother drive down Forfar's Main Street in a Rolls-Royce I was sick in as a child. Behind me the watercolours of stick girls walking through trees are misted blobs percolating in coffee steam. Mother comes in like Scott of the Antarctic carrying tents of shopping. The garçon brings a cappucino and croissants on which she wields her knife with the off-frantic precision of violins in Hitchcock's shower scene. Soon I will tell her. Show her dust in the sugar spoon. Her knife gouges craters in the dough like an ice-axe and she tells the story of nineteen Siberian ponies she queued behind in the supermarket. Of Captain Oates who boxed her fallen 'Ariel'. The chocolate from the cappucino has gone all over her saucer. There is a scene and silence. Now tell her. Tell her above the coffee table which scrapes with the masked voice of a pier seeming to let in some waters, returning others to the sea, diverting the pack-ice which skirts around its legs. Tell her a fact about you she knows but does not know and which you will tell her except that the surviving ponies are killed and the food depot named Desolation Camp made from their carcasses keeps getting in the way. From this table we will write postcards, make wireless contact with home and I will tell her of King Edward VII Land, of how I have been with Dr Wilson and then alone, so alone, in day-blizzards just eleven miles short of the Pole and ask her to follow me. I am afraid she has been there already. She smiles like the Great Beardmore Glacier and goes out into the street with stick girls to the thirty-four sledgedogs and the motor-sledges. You are too late. Amundsen is in Forfar. She has an appointment. Behind me I can sense the canvases, the dried grasses pressed into their grain like eczema on an open palm. Later I will discover her diary and what I told her.

HOHENZENGGESTECH

A joust of peace (gestech) to be distinguished from a joust of war (rennen). The opponents were made easier targets for each other by sitting in high saddles. The object was to break lances on your opponent rather than to unhorse and kill him.

With data gloves you place it
Like a crown upon your head;
With both hands ease the vizor
Down: it smells of joust
And with your tongue you flick
At embossed foliage, breathe
Condensation on the underside
Of slashing. In this white
Sheath of armour you're safe:
The Greek root of prophylactic.

It grows on you: cutlet, greave,
Mail hauberk glint in the house
Music of this dungeon
And through the haze of ecstasy
You mark your man.

He fancies tasset, your
Cuisse, your shapely sabaton.
His besagews strobe like eyes.
You grow a horse. You pick out
Words – *Ave, Maria, Ave Domine* –
On ribs riveted to the right.
You close upon the fluting
Of his coif.

Its a sin the music sings;
There is no breach for friends.
Yet when the clock strikes three
And you hang your suit up
In its kelvingrove of glass,
You notice how it smells
Of blood, stale semen, a quick
But clinging smoke.

BEES

When those raftered bees
mistook our bed for hives,
explored the runnelled comb
of sheets and arching legs
gone limewood in our sleep,

when they began to fabricate
among the mesh of hair and flesh,
small changes caught at
the corners of our room
which curled like paper
in a matchstick flame.

Sun-showers shone through the walls,
veined wings of berried stucco
flaked and fell upon the bed.

In wallets of our jackets
snaps of people that we knew too well
relaxed their frames,
allowing them to smile,
remember us as we never were to them.

And then we woke
with the same premonition
of a garden entering our room,
a queen bee on its threshold
with maps of its geography
traced in pollen on her wings.

HUZZIEBAW

Hush-a-baa or huzziebaw: *a lullaby from the verb to huzzh.*
S. pron. with so strong a sibillation that it cannot properly be
expressed in writing. Clips attached to the H and W enable
you to fasten it around your head as with all middle-alphabet
words. Select your preferred definition by pressing firmly on
the hyphens: impelled by the sea-saw of its own intimate
history, huzziebaw will balance between your eyebrows and
take over:

mantelpiece clocks in the fragrant Dinard light tick past you
like lemons on an old fruit machine: hush-a-baa.

aluminium trolleys forward and reverse in the quiet green
hospice: huzziebaw

the landscape steadies and you see a young man lying with
purple marks all over his thin body, a mother and sister
kneeling, a man, who is his lover, poised, and a photo-
grapher, crouched. We are all waiting. This is huzziebaw.
And you wonder: surely the closed curtains swaying in the
summer air will bring forth something: ease, a scrap of
melody, a brittle word that will not simply say the pain of
this last lullaby but be it, blinding us beyond the reach of the
camera's ultimate, pale cut.

THE TEST

They carry you to a precipice of niceness
And smile like hammocks. My friend
Watches them search out good findable
Veins, listens peaceably as they sigh
Stories of 'others' who have injected theirs
To kingdom come. You have come with him
As to an ark, stare briefly into the purest
Trust you'll ever know, wondering if, in park
Or garden, you betrayed each other when merely
Strangers, destined to meet, months before this room.

WARMER BRUDER

A slang expression, literally 'hot brothers', used viciously of homosexuals in the death camps of Sachsenhausen and Flossenburg.

i
Concentrate hot brothers:
Shovel snow with me
In Sachsenhausen
From one side to the other
And back again.

Then in the silence
Make an angel of the snow
Which falls unceasingly
On camp and foe.

The lights of Grangemouth
Dance their triangles
Into tears,
Its smoke the ghost of blood,
The melting snow.

ii
Concentrate hot brothers:
Make an angel of the snow
And shovel Sachsenhausen
Silence from one side to the other
And back again.

O warmer bruder
Tonight you fall
Shaping car windows
With triangles of Grangemouth light.

Smoke, the ghost of blood,
Fills up the melting sky.

iii
Blood dropped on Sachsenhausen
Snow was silenced,
Shoveled out of history.
But here in Scotland
It does not melt

And cloaks the Grangemouth
Sky with red triangles.
This is no sunset
But concentrated smoke
That stings the eye.

iv
Triangles of smoke
Blood the Grangemouth skies.
Along the Forth the hospice
Workers shovel snow

From drives that keep the patients
Bound, while silence, like an angel,
Visits and stays on.

THREE WEE FREES
To John MacLeod

I HINNIE-PIGS
(or Wan wee free)

thur wiz this wee free rite
an hi wiz doazin aff in a pew
wi the meenister goan on'n'on

sittin oan hiz hauns hi wiz
jist like at school when hi pleyed
hinnie-pigs. hinnie-pigs

wiz when wan o the boys
tried tae lift ye up by thi
oxters an gave ye three shakes.

if yer hauns went aw flabby like
ye wur a rite wersh wee git
an a bent shot intae thi bargain!

a woofter man! if yer hauns
steyed pit ye wur a hinnie-pot or
pig an *youz* got a shot at thi liftin.

wull. thur wiz this wee free rite
sittin tite oan hiz hauns
skretchin his erse as hi snoozed

dreemin o hinnie-pigs when
all o a sudden its Jeezusiz' turn.
Aye Jeezus! Christ! hi seez Jeezus

dayin sum liftin. Jeezus thi hinnie-

merchant feelin fur sweet oxters an
sour yins. wull blow me if hi didni

chooz thi biggest harry hoof
o thi lot! am tellin ye hiz hauns
wur everywher. bloody whirligig hi wiz.

an thi wee free wiz fair gobsmacked
when hi jalouzed that thi guy doin
thi jack'n'thi boax wiz thi wee free

hisel an Jeezus seyin tae him: it's yoor
turn noo son. it's thi nippy sweetie's turn.

II   LOT

(or Anither wee free)

thur wiz this wee free rite
name o Lot wi a wifie missus Lot
an two braw lassies

steyed up a close in thi Drum
pure mental they wur
tell ye why: wan day

Lot wiz haen a hingie
jist back fae thi broo
thi missus layin it aff

tae him aboot this an that
when all o a sudden hi sees
angels o thi lord

daunerin doon thi road
wi a bunch o buggers

gien em thi glad eye.

oot pops Lot an gobsmacks
thi hail shabang: disnae
stoap tae ask hisel if thi fowk

are angels an buggers
or which is which
but bundles thi wans wi wings

up thi close an offers
his weans tae thi ithers
heavenly logic eh? weel

thi buggers didne hae time
tae get ower thi shock cause
Lot wiz oot wi a chain-saw

two minutes eftir. he got
Bar-L an thi missus wiz turned
tae a pillar o salt.

III THI LAST WEE FREE

thur wiz this wee free rite
doon in Glesca fur a day
at thi virtual reality shoap

esks fur a new testament
vizor an turns up romans
1,27: ye ken thi bit aboot

men dayin 'shamfu things' wi ither
men. Paul caas em 'bangsters'
'scorners' 'sleekie' an 'ill-hairtit'

an thi wee free wiz expectin
a bit o stonin at thi verra least
men o God pittin oot sum ees

when all o a sudden whit duz hi see
but Davie an Eric oan thir knees
afore thi lord hisel hauns joined

thegither makin vows. aye. an thi
Christ Jeezus blessin an smilin
sayin: 'Lat him at hes lugs in his

heid hairken'. black affrontit
thi wee free wiz. complained
tae thi mainiger an goat hiz

reddies back: thirty pieces o siller.

MAMAPOULES

Perhaps the end began
On a sun-deck in the Caribbean:
Liming with you in Barbadan
Shade I watched you slip

Asleep, your senses tousled by the constant
Wash of sea and surf and listened
To my silence with you begin.
How will I say it,

Sing it, so that even sun-tanned
Loungers will sit up
At a tale of *mamapoules*,
One well, the other ill

With a virus, shapely and complex
As the reef that built this island?
No simple elegy wipes the smirk
Or stare from faces when they twig.

Only our guide, Adolphus Job,
Laughs *with* us, jabbed
Against the prejudice that shipped
His forbears here. In our red hair

He finds a wisp of white
Perjonnies whose Scottish
Misdemeanour earned Atlantic
Breakers. Not for them the Caribbean

Side of sugar clubs, green
Pitches of fast-bowling snorklers;

Simply 'Windward parishes' of shifting
Sand they christened 'Scotland'.

Now as then we seek a tongue
To mark this difference
And listen to Job's patient
Chatter with the driver

Of our tourist bus: a dialect
Whose English grammar's strung
With the surf of unfamiliar
Words: some, forgotten Scots,

Some African, most a bevelled
English slurred by sun
And contempt for tyranny.
He 'visits us de Plantation House',

Points out 'de doctor-booby hummin
At de cotton-tree', 'chats
Down' the ticket girls
In a slang that's semi-

Rural seasoned with urban
Patois. It tugs at our
Ears like a sea that's toured
Beach traders' conches.

Anemone of laid-back
Syllables, part time, part
Space, its words are tiny
Genes of sound encoding

Colours, difference, a music
Out of step with 'progress'
And so aborted, exiled,

Enslaved with the folk that spoke them.

Now the master race on holiday
Can't understand its own tongue
Talking back to it:
Black vowels, convicted consonants,

Queer as the politeness of their hosts.

My friend is 'going home to die':
He steers a *redleg* charter
Slowly through the reefs of dialect
And dives against advice,

Keeps on his rings whose glint
Attracts the barracuda.
A young wreck at sixty feet
Swims through his goggles:

A fishing boat aged twenty-one
Blown up for dollars
And underwater cameras.
He'll surface any moment

Now with a swish of airport
Doors: too fast and the bends
Will jinx his tongue,
His English shattered

Like his body by refracted
Sunlight in the water.

Liming – idling. mamapoule - a gay man. perjonnie – a
white, Scots deportee. doctor booby – humming bird.
chat down – chat up. redleg – a poor, white Barbadan,
originally an indentured servant.

DR DAVID KYNALOCHUS
IN LE PENSIONNAT D'HUMMING-BIRD GARDEN

A green old age, Fate grant us each,
Me, without law, you, without leech!

Kynalochus, *De Hominis Procreatione*

About Dr David Kynalochus (1559-1617)

"Little is known of Kinloch beyond his authorship of Latin verse. The verses were published in Paris in 1596 and reprinted in *Delitiae Poetarum Scotorum* in 1637, and his first book, *De Hominis Procreatione*, makes Kinloch the first Scottish writer on obstetrics. He was born in Dundee, "incorporated" at the University in St Andrews in 1576, but did not graduate. In 1596 he was M.D., probably of Paris, where he was well known as devoted to the study of anatomy. Tradition has it that he was called to give medical service at the Court. Kinloch travelled a great deal and on one journey in Spain he was seized by the Inquisition and condemned to auto-da-fé. Tradition again has it that when the execution was delayed he made enquiry and was told that the Grand Inquisitor was ill and he must wait. Making use of a friendly black cat to bear his message he made known his status and offered his service. This was accepted, the Grand Inquisitor recovered, and Kinloch was sent home to illuminate his native land."

The present author is no relation of Dr David Kynalochus.

Source: R. C. Buist, "Dr David Kinloch (Kynalochus)", *The British Medical Journal*, May 1, 1926, p. 793. I am indebted to Dr. John Durkan of Glasgow University for making this information available to me.

ITEM: *creed*, no juist the same as the Inquisitor's. *Colour*:
owre white (owre reid tae be a *legal* immigrant). *Medecine*:
alien, 'morisco' même (cause eh complouter baith auld *an*
new). The morn they'll burn it oot o me wi ither witches (wha's
pleesure ligs i young lads erses). Me! David Kynalochus, M.D.,
Dundee, Montpellier, the furst wha pit obstetrics intae Latin
metrics! ITEM: *morality*: fremmit (tharefore queer). ITEM:
Me! David Kynalochus wha tousled oot the dauphin fae the
tappietourie o the French Queen's wame. Och! the plague
bumbazes ivry wan o us: inquisitor an heretic alike suspeck
maist human contact, aa queerosity a sign o blude-born viruses
that sauchtly colonize syne pox us tae oblivion. Plain daft
though tae think as thae releegious dae: they'd chirk meh body
fae meh saul despite the Guid Buik whilk commands respeck
fur blude. Auld Moses says: 'Sanguis est ipsissima vita'. Pit
siller intae blude an yi wull sauf the saul. Pitifu Inquisitor, *mon
semblable, mon frère*! The virr o life's agin him tae: the swallie
swalls an toxoplasma gondii gilravage aa his body's humours.
Remeid's beyond meh ken, but faither's auncient airt wi
herbs micht bring sum easement. Oh, if eh cud hap him lyk a
bee in het aise o pennyroyal eh wud see Scoatlan afore the
month wiz oot! A but shell brunt an thirled tae thi hinside o
his heid wad turn his gray een bleck. Whut wull he leir? The
sonsieness o equilibrium, that eh, though different, am the
semm as him, oor intimmers siclike, oor airteries lyk poly-shee
that fesh up prison watter. ITEM: eftir the taur an featherin, the
sack, the cauld white cake o eldin placed i trummlin hauns,
ITEM, yi wull smell flours an herbs amang the faggots, succory
or lad's love, dill or dent-de lyon: a hum fae Scoatlan, curative,
memorial. In orcharts by Dundee, eh'll shaw yi, ITEM, dreels o
healin names, a quilt o herbs, mind how yi smile i sunlicht, ruit
the yird wi spunk an salve the guilt o aa yi touch.

APARINE

Aparine siue Philanthropus, siue Omphacocarpos is called in english goosgrasse or Goosehareth, in Duche Klebkraute, in frenche Grateron, the herbe scoureth away and dryeth.

In June 1981, the Centers for Disease Control in Atlanta, Georgia receives its first reports of a relatively rare form of pneumonia, pneumocystis carinii pneumonia (PCP) and of outbreaks of Kaposi's sarcoma in young men. PCP was common amongst those liberated from concentration camps in Europe at the end of the Second World War.

BARBARE HERBA

Berbare herba groweth aboute Brokes and water sydes. It hath leaues lyke Rocket, wherefore it maye be called in englishe wound-rocket for it is good for a wounde. Some cal thys Carpentariam.

NEEDLEPOINT

Injecting your name
Through this soft quilt
With thread as red as blood,
I remember my domestic science grades
And stop.

I try to pass you through the eye
But everything dissolves in water.

Just as everything is free:
I can give you moons or oranges.
The words you kept up like spinning plates,
Reinvent your signature.
Who will know but me.

Now my jongleur is in stitches
On this tapestry
And it is your smile
I wrap up in this flag.

It covers green fields when unfolded,
Its nations visited by grieving
Elderly in golf buggies and on bicycles,
A thing of shreds and patches,
Moveable Passchendaele.

Yet I'm scared that in the night
I'll stretch out beneath my quilt
And will not find you among the names,
And turn to others, tongue-tied,
Who travel further every year
Seeking their own small country.

CYTISUS

Cytisus groweth plentuously in mount Appennine, I haue had it growyng in my gardine in high Germany, I haue not sene it in Englande. Cytisus may be called in englishe tretrifoly.

THE DAY OF SAINT COLUMBA
adapted from Alexander Carmichael

Thursday of Saint Columba benign
Day to draw up the sheet upon his face
Day to zip up the green body-bag
Day to disinfect his bed.

Day to discard my plastic gloves
Day to collect his personal effects
Day to return the oxygen mask
Day to sleep and sleep

Day to converse with florists
Day to phone friends
Day of my beloved, the Thursday
Day of my beloved, the Thursday

The main structural constituents of HIV are:
-core proteins, derived from the Gag *gene, which form the main internal structure of the virus. The most widely studied of these is known as* p24.

-envelope glycoproteins, derived from the env *gene, which cover the surface of the virus and play an important role in the interaction between virus and host cell. HIV envelope glycoproteins known as* gp160, gp120 *and* gp41 *also appear on the surface of infected cells and may therefore play a role in the spread of infection from cell to cell and in disease development;*

-enzymes derived from the pol *gene which catalyse a number of biochemical reactions in the virus life-cycle. The known enzymes are* reverse transcriptase (RT), protease, endonuclease *and* ribonuclease H; *all are possible targets for anti-viral drugs. In addition, there are a number of small proteins known as regulatory proteins which play a role in controlling and coordinating the events of the virus life cycle. These are derived from genes with code names such as* TAT, REV, VIF, NEF.

EPHEMERUM NON LETHALE

Ephemeru is called in duche meyblumle, in french Muguet. It groweth plentuously in Germany, but not in England that ever I could see, sauynge in my Lordes gardine at Syon. The poticaries in Germany do name it Lilium couallium, it may be called in englishe May Lillies.

NAMES

Now a kind of flesh is given back
To names which wasted, to all the signs
Of life in Bernard, Tom, in Kurt and David:
Four dogs, a kite, balloons, some last words stitched

In bubbles, imprint their shapes on damp October
Grass: we watch them soak in Washington dew.
At sunset, then, the quilt is thrown back
And tied in bales; the earth shows up a skein

Of patches as if wild deer had pressed it
Into sleep. Again we kneel and run
Our fingers over still warm squares:
Our short-term sons have just stepped out beyond

The field of vision and may be called to
Among the dark paths of White House lawns.

FRAGRARIA

*Fragraria is called in english a strawbery leafe, whose fruite is
called in englishe a strawbery, in duche Erdeber, in frenche
Fraysne. Euery man knoweth wel inough where strawberies
growe.*

The synthesis of all the HIV proteins and consequent produc-
tion of viral particles is controlled by a region of the HIV
genome known as the long terminal repeat (LTR). Much
effort, by many laboratories, has therefore focused on factors
which might influence activity of the LTR.

A CHEVAL

The endless small light of the ward
Spooled out his breath and breath:

A reeling, a casting off, taught thread
Relaxed and then convulsively pulled
In to your smart finger;

A remembering, a forgetting, the clock's
Calm bobbin pulling you around
Its wooden grumbling centre

Saying: safe now, a new pattern
Sews in the fabric as easily
As the flowers your fingers grow for him.

Until the tearing anger unwinds itself
Because it is all stitched, all sewn up.

You prick your finger
Sleep for a hundred years
Wake up, older by one square foot.

LITTLE QUAKING GRASS

Here then is my finger lullaby
Pushing gently and withdrawing,
Dolphining upon this quilt,
The trough and wave of cotton.

I hem your red boat with borders
And watch you sail on Washington grass,
Whipping a green wake beneath you.

At dusk the park attendants rake
Out your ocean: dandelions,
The usual chains of memory,
But also unexpected herbs
In all the languages we loved:

Showy clover for my dustie-fute,
Kleines liebesgras,
Love-lies-bleeding,
And live-forever,
Kleines zittergras.

GOSSIPIUM

Gossipiu is called of Barbarus wryters, Bombax and Cononum, in englishe Coton, in greeke Pylon, in duche Baumewoll, in frenche ducotton. I never sawe it growyng sauying onely in Bonony.

THE BARNACLE GOOSE

The loom was fireproof larch
Berthed in my morning room.

I plucked a cat's cradle
From its awkward hull
And it climbed my arms like rigging.

Later, I took a candle,
And in its crisp flame
Pebbledash stubble
Of feathered barnacle
Mottled the rotting timber;

A shell cracked in the night,
Air rose in a plume
And the loom swung like a hammock.

HALIMUS

*Halimus groweth plentuously in the Ilandes of east
Freselande where as the inhabitants make veriuce of the red
beries. I haue sene it also in Flaunders by the sea syde. It may
be called in englishe sea wyllowe or prickwylowe because it
hath the leaves of a wylowe and prickes lyke a thorne.*

LOVE CHARM
adapted from Alexander Carmichael

I took the foxglove
And the butterbur
To the broad flat flag

And sowed them in your silk

I cut nine stems of ferns
I took three lucky bones
From an old man's grave

And stitched them in your silk

I held your patch of quilt
Against the morning light

Against the sting of the north wind

And I will pledge and warrant you
This man will never leave you

CUMMA

When they asked me
What sign would sew you up,
I remembered foam
Inverting brown legs
Through the Caribbean green;

And so I ordered you
A manx-man's leg that brought
Up blue *memento-mori:*

The laughter of rose
Shivering fish caught
In the pouch of swimming trunks.

I identify the body:
'Da sea en got
No back door boy'.

Cumma – come on! come here!

You thread a sea with your eye;
Each time the needle enters your flank
The pain composes you;

Trees that hung your voice
Among their patterns
Wrap your quilt in foliage;

A dog barks through the branches;
A girl's arm passes like an oar
Across the sunlit patches;

Now your song kneels
At the river's edge
And will not flow;

Your passport head is pinned in silk.

Speech fails and so you turn the brightness thumbwheel up. Shift. Backspace. The screen's green loom displays a printfield of mnemonics, hard spaces, limbo, an *acre-braid* of good housekeeping unravelled by a virus. Stitches drop: the *n's* and *d's*, the *p's* of plosives where we lived and now a young man stands with clumsy scissors before the template he's been given. Cut. Paste. Close up in feet of cotton the story of your love. You remember passwords but their spelling's queer, each one disabled by a cross of obsolescence. And yet it's with this needle that he sews, this bar of light, enabling memories, centring the yarn upon the screen. Now watch the herb doctor coalescing on the Caribbean sheen, Kynalochus *passmenter*, Dundee *braboner* and *dustie-fute*. He dances on a net of words he isolates like glycoproteins, warps *gp41*, racks *160* with a *herrin band* and opens up a tiny jesp to jink at the gene beneath. *Tat, rev, viv, nef* are plucked like harp strings from the loom and fall as *pob-tow* to the ground: regulatory proteins, refuse of flax, *thrums* that reek of vervain, rue and thyme, the shuttle's long terminal repeat cut to a measure fitting us. Then, when the *fleeing tailor* lets his quilt touch grass, I know how to live in you and tear *greengown* from your shoulders. Here is the word which is the turf I weep on and the loss of our virginity in open air. A *joram* sung by the *alamouti* crosses the waters of your coat, the air a *huzziebaw* of voices murmuring coloured names. All the old words come back, *snoove* through *aethiopus*, and with them the earth and all we lost when the loom flickered in our fingers. That day *froe* fell like muzzy seed from White House trees and so you stretched your trampoline beneath it and scratched our names upon the sky. *Rinker* leapt a stallion leap of grief into a silky sea and there he rides now, a blue horse in a patch of red neighing the

Renfrew Ferry. The *amplefeyst* is stilled. The scrape of my *abstraklous* pen a pin that's *surfling* in a hem. And now as you sleep beneath this quilt, dandelion, *dent-de-lyon*, *pish-the bed* and *what o'clock*, each in their different accents tell the time by your sure breath. It is eternal *lempit-ebb*: you kneel on a shore between two tides, the cloth waves gently into knuckles kneeding the small of his back, the hollow of his throat.

MALUS

Malus is named in greke Melea, in englishe an Apple tree, in duche Ein Opfel baume, in french Vn pommier.

CAT QUIXOTE

Cat tilts his way to Grand's four poster: a tabloid mosquito net of LESBIAN TEACHER HORROR is whipped about the bed by ceiling fans and Cat and Grand share sway together. Grand snoozes and struggles in his snooze with something black: prickly heat from heckiebirnie scribbling from his toes, stalled air, THE SCANDAL OF GAY VICARS. Grand stretches on his plank, weaves deeper into dream. Its loom casts off. A heretic buzzes at his ear. Cat slips a leaf of sage beneath Grand's pillow and with dry, tiny licks wipes wrinkles from his brow, lets lashes chase about his face, each cil just separate yet touching, apart but free as pupils still beneath their lids. Cat Quixote gives the Grand Inquisitor windmill eyes: the gift of tasting clearly portions of the air where each brown arm has swung, the equality of all points on a circle. 'The bed is not flat, your Grace', Cat Quixote purrs, 'It's rigging bends like the cotton plant which spun your sheets and in the morning sun it hatches out an animal of fleece: a queer white lamb grazing the pasture of your disbelief'.

PENELOPE

Now the shuttle is becalmed
And out in the loom
The red cotton boat unravels
About the bobbin. I draw
The longed-for ship of thread
Towards me and it disappears.

I am only happy in the night
When the day's patchwork
Is undone and I begin again
To dream our life, free of the silver
Needle that shoots you far from me
Into simple memory.

But then I must cast-off again,
My finger pointing like a seal's
Head towards the sun,
Then spiralling into tissue which falls
Away from my knees
Like the torn fabric of your sail.

With pins between pursed lips
And stuck in cuffs I would sew
Myself into the myth I weave
For you, board our boat
And slip forever the loom's dark jetty.

DR DAVID KYNALOCHUS IN LE PENSIONNAT
D'HUMMING-BIRD GARDEN

*He feels Scotland at his wrists like cool water on a hot day.
Steadily it beats its freshness into his writing hand and a snail
of laughter tugs back his lips; fine traceries of sand dishevel
his face. Vermeer's geographer has this intentness and on the
seventh floor of Le Pensionnat d'Humming-Bird Garden,
Kynalochus is planning a Scottish world. It must have -his
compass tells him- the rapt attention of a diving bell at
20,000 feet. Each square centimetre of pressure on its skin of
cloud and mountain must not be left to chance. It must have
the terrible desire of a fly sucking sky into its feet through
glass, he thinks, and its margin of western light must be
bevelled from the fast space a bird folds away in its wings.
What will it be for, he asks? For quick calculation, invention
and the cryptic exclamation mark. As a chaser for all desire.
For healing: an Iona of plain space where language may draw
breath and, poised before its flock of pattering significances,
dilute portions of weather into its unstable spirit. For healing:
an orphanage of words where a child parries the butterflies in
a big man's beard with that violent question 'What is grass?'
and instead of a word thrown back at him in simple baffle-
ment, a word falling useless among tall grasses, raises his
head, his eyes and nostrils wild with the word GRASS! In Le
Pensionnat d'Humming-Bird Garden, Kynalochus invents all
the Scotlands. He chooses his words, not for their vowels, not
for their consonants, but for the barely visible scaffolding of
wild herbs that support them. His compass moves like a
spider along the airy crossbeams of convolvulus and prunes
his nouns of absence. A dustie-fute, an acrobat, miles from
home, he feels for the first time in centuries the pain of his
land strike up through his language like an absent flower.*

GLOSSARY

ableeze	ablaze
abstraklous	obstreperous
acre-braid	the breadth of an acre
afftak	a piece of waggery
aftercome	consequence
aise	ashes
ait-seed	oat seed
amplefeyst	a fit of the sulks or spleen; needless talk
baghash	abuse with the tongue
bairnie of the e'e	the pupil of the eye
bellum	noise
ben	inner part; mountain
birk	tree
bobbin-quaw	a quaking bog
bouk	body
braboner	weaver
broo	job centre
bumbaze	confuse, befuddle
burd-bouky	full of birds
by-coming	passing by
chiel	a man
chirk	grate
close	tenement close or entrance
complouter	mix
cream o thi well	the first water drawn from a well on Ne'er's Day

dauner	stroll
dounmaist	lowest
een	eyes
eldin	firelighter
end-pickle	head of corn
esh	ash
ezle	a spark of fire; a hot ember
falderall	a gewgaw, a useless ornament, a pedantic, giddy person
fesh up	fetch up, pull up
fire-edge	the first eagerness or heat
fleechit	flattered
fleeing tailor	travelling tailor
fore	privilege
flow	quicksand
flush	a marshy place, blossom, a large flow of milk from cows
freen	friend
fremmit	foreign
froe	sperm
fullyerie	foliage
galations	a boys' Christmas mime play
greengown	the loss of virginity in the open air; sod, turf on a grave
habbacraws	an expression of suspense, the precise meaning of which now escapes me
hairken	listen
hap	wrap

hay a hingie	hang idly out of the window and gossip with neighbours
herrin band	a string dividing cuts or heeres of yarn into separate bundles
heugh	crag, cliff
hinnie-merchant	honey-merchant
hoburn sauch	laburnum
hubble	uproar, tumult
huzzibaw	lullaby
icker	ear of corn
intimmers	innards
jalouze	realize
jesp	a small gap; a flaw in the weave of fabric, a broken thread
jink	move jerkily to and fro as when spinning
kaim	comb
laggery	miry
learn	teach
lempit-ebb	the shore between high and low tide where limpets are gathered
lent fever craig	a slow feverish throat
lently	slowly
let abee	not to mention, omit
lowe	flame
lugs	ears
lytach	a large mass of wet substance; speech in an unknown tongue; a long rambling piece of news; a long disconnected piece of literature

mou	mouth
mump the cuddie	a children's game
murloch	the young dogfish
mynd	to remember

nippy sweetie	effeminate man

outloup	to leap out
outpour	a downpour of rain or snow
oxter	armpit

painch	stomach
pasmentar	a passement weaver
plouter	to wade through water or mud
pob-tow	refuse of flax
polly-shee	pulleys
printfield	cotton-printing works

rale	real
redd	brush
remeid	remedy
roarin-buckie	a kind of shell

scrieve	write
shabang	lot
shirpit	mean; here: pointed
skeer	sheer
snood	a ribbon or band for confing the hair; a twist of temper
snoove	twist, twirl, spin
souch	a hollow murmuring sound; a deep sigh,

	restless sleep
spunk	guts, courage
steek the gab	keep silent
stour	stir, bustle, chaff, a cloud of spray, a smoke-like fog
straik	stroke
stravaig	roam up and down
summer-cloks	sunbeams
surfle	gather, ruck a hem
swallie swalls	lymph glands swell
taigle	to tarry, loiter, dawdle
tappietourie	a knob of pastry over the centre-hole in a pie; something which rises to a peak, a mound
thrums	threads
transmeridiane	the region beyond the meridian in the Atlantic which separates the new from the old world
wame	womb
wersh	sour
whileoms	sometimes
wider-gleam	any cold or exposed place on an eminence
yawl	boat